D0290663

Perfect Peace and Rest

FEATURING *the* ARTWORK *of*

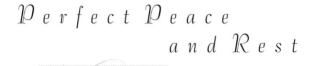

THOMAS KINKADE

Published in Nashville, Tennessee,
by Thomas Nelson, Inc., Publishers.

ISBN 0-7852-6708-5

Printed in the United States of America
1 2 3 4 5 6 7—06 05 04 03 02 01

$\mathcal{P}$ erfect $\mathcal{P}$ eace
and $\mathcal{R}$ est

FEATURING *the* ARTWORK *of*

THOMAS
KINKADE

THOMAS NELSON PUBLISHERS®

Nashville

Thomas Kinkade

Home Sweet Home

*Lord, you have been
our dwelling place
throughout all generations.
Before the mountains were
born or you brought forth
the earth and the world,
from everlasting to
everlasting you are God.*
Psalm 90:1–2 (NIV)

I remember well the day my parents dropped me off at college. We spent the day fixing up my dorm room, shopping for just the right bedspread, and hanging up posters and all other accoutrements to make my small space feel like home. I remember the moment after we said our good-byes as I watched them drive off. I watched until I could no longer see the taillights as they turned eastward, heading home. I felt an emptiness in the pit of my stomach. A restlessness seized me that I couldn't shake. As I walked back into my new room, I felt like a stranger in a foreign land. Nothing seemed familiar. The faces were all different, the place out of context. This was not home—home was eight hundred miles away where my family was returning. I didn't belong here.

Of course, it was only a matter of time before my small room became home, and over the course of four years, the college campus and my community of friends there replaced my childhood home as the place where I most belonged. We all long for that sense of "home" and belonging. For each one of us, there is that place, either real or imagined, present or past, that evokes that sense of home. Yet, earthly homes are finite and constantly changing. Friends with whom we connect move away. Job transfers and career changes dictate an unwanted move. Children leave to find their own "space" in this world. And what is left but that empty, restless feeling of not belonging, of loss, of adjusting to yet another change that life inevitably brings?

Thankfully, as believers, we can rejoice with the psalmist in Psalm 90 that, "Lord, through all the generations you have been our home!" (NLT). No matter where we are in our life experiences, no matter what changes inevitably approach, God remains constant. Throughout the generations, God provides a place where we find rest and comfort, a place where we can belong, a place that we can call home. I have at times experienced that same emptiness and restlessness I felt that first day of college. But now I have the assurance that there is no place on earth, no place I can be in my life, where God is not always with me. I have learned to make every place a resting place because I am always "at home" with my God.

- *Betsy Schmitt*

Dear Lord, thank You that throughout all generations, You are our true home. Our life circumstances may change, and our address may not always be the same, but wherever we are and wherever we go, You go before us to provide a place of comfort and rest, a place we can call home. Help us to keep our hearts and faces focused homeward on You throughout the challenges and changes that our lives bring. In Your unchanging name we pray, amen.

Peace Where You Live

❧

*For the Kingdom of God is
not a matter of what we eat
or drink, but of living a life
of goodness and peace and
joy in the Holy Spirit.
If you serve Christ with this
attitude, you will please God.
And other people will
approve of you, too.
So then, let us aim for
harmony in the church and
try to build each other up.*

Romans 14:17–19 (NLT)

John Donne wrote, "No man is an island." No one lives in total isolation. Even if we spend most of our time apart from others, we have contact points with other people, whether it's the clerk at the local grocery store or the voice on the phone asking you to subscribe to the local newspaper. We all live in community, whether our surroundings are a small rural farm town, an upscale beach resort, a classic suburban neighborhood with two-car garages and neatly manicured lawns, or an "urbanscape" with the intensified press of humanity never far away. As Christians, we are called to live in community. "And let us not neglect our meeting together, as some people do, but encourage and warn each other, especially now that the day of his coming back again is drawing near" (Heb. 10:25 NLT). The question then becomes, how do we live in community?

Paul is very clear on this point. He writes in Romans 14:17–19 that the Christian's attitude of living should be one of righteousness, peace, and joy. Our aim should be to live in harmony with each other and to encourage one another. We need look no further than the front page of the daily newspaper, though, to see that we have not come very far in learning how to live in peace with those around us. Wars, whose origins date back thousands of years, still rage. Racial strife still boils, despite laws that proclaim otherwise. We need not travel long on the roads before we encounter drivers whose idea of living in harmony is cutting

others off so that they can reach their destinations more quickly. Is it any wonder that at times we would like to be isolated, alone on an island?

With whom are you in community? Is it the neighbor who lets his dog dig up your garden every spring? Or the church member on your ministry team who insists that there is only one way to do things—his way? Or the coworker who somehow always manages to direct the tough projects to your desk? Maybe it's the family member who believes the world revolves around her needs. We will never escape the fact that we are in community with a lot of people who are just plain difficult. Whatever the situation, though, our call remains the same. We are to live in harmony with a spirit of peace. Our model is Jesus, and the key is acceptance. "So accept each other just as Christ has accepted you; then God will be glorified" (Rom. 15:7 NLT).

Maybe we cannot change the world, or even our close community. But we can bring an attitude of goodness, joy, and peace to the place where we live right now.

- *Betsy Schmitt*

Dear Lord, thank You for the Spirit's gifts of goodness, joy, and peace. Help us through the Holy Spirit to live in community with that same attitude, bringing harmony and acceptance to those around us. Amen.

Working Peace

Turn away from evil

and do good.

Work hard at living

in peace with others.

1 Peter 3:11 (NLT)

Every summer my family takes a vacation toward the end of July, in that small window of time after summer activities conclude and before school activities begin. We have done a number of different vacations—we visited historical sites, such as Williamsburg and Monticello, took a family car trip out west, and spent time in the mountains. But what we look forward to most are the vacations when we spend one or two weeks at the beach. That long stretch of powdery white sand along the west coast of Florida is one place where I can fully unwind and return home restored and refreshed.

But I work hard for those respites from the daily routine. Not only do I need to put my time in at work to earn vacation time, but I also need to work through a long list of "to do's" before we even walk out the door. It sounds like this: Finish last-minute details at work, write out careful instructions for the neighbor boy who is going to water the plants, take the dog to the kennel, do the final loads of laundry so that everyone has the right clothes to pack, pack, and then clean the car out for the trip. It's an exhausting, stressful process (just ask my family!), but when vacation comes, the process is inevitable. Once we arrive, we unpack the car and head for the beach. There is no question, though, that all that work was well worth the end result.

Living at peace with others is much the same—it is a worthwhile goal that requires great effort. In other words, we need to work at peace, just as Peter writes.

Too often, we consider peacemaking a passive role. But a skilled peacemaker actively seeks peace by working to establish good relationships, by keeping communication lines open, by resolutely dealing with conflicts, and by bringing the issues out in the open rather than ignoring them until it's too late. The effective peacemaker anticipates problems and purposefully deals with them before they occur.

In what areas of your life do you need to work hard to keep the peace? Maybe you need to take a more active role in keeping the lines of communication open between yourself and a child or yourself and your spouse. Perhaps you have a coworker who is difficult to work with. How can you be proactive in heading off conflicts in that relationship? In every aspect of our lives, we need peacemaking skills. Without question, living at peace will require extra work and commitment. But like that first glimpse of the beach, the reward of peace will be well worth the effort.

- *Betsy Schmitt*

Father, You call us to be peacemakers. Help us to see clearly the relationships and the situations where we need to work at living in peace with others. Equip us through Your Holy Spirit to do the necessary things to bring about peace rather than conflict. Amen.

Pure Rest

Be at rest once more,
O my soul,
for the *LORD* has
been good to you.
For you, O *LORD*,
have delivered my soul
from death, my eyes
from tears, my feet
from stumbling,
that I may walk
before the *LORD*
in the land of the living.

Psalm 116:7–9 (NIV)

The sweetest rest follows periods of great exertion. Following a winding, steeply climbing trail through dense forest, the day hiker is rewarded by an incredible ocean vista opening out before her. The goal has been reached. Now she can spread out a blanket, enjoy a picnic, and relax. The same can be said of any objective in our lives for which we earnestly strive. When the effort has been expended, we can look with satisfaction upon our accomplishments and enjoy their fruits.

Also, true rest requires an underlying sense that all is well. Certainly, the limitations of our mortal minds, bodies, and spirits may require that we cease our striving from time to time in order to regroup. But this does not exemplify the purest rest we seek. When we find momentary rest, the challenges and perils yet await us. Once we have slept or meditated or had some "down time," we must resume the quest. This kind of rest is marred by the anticipation of renewed struggle. Indeed, this kind of temporary rest may be interrupted unceremoniously by the very challenges that drive us on.

True rest is one of the great rewards of following God. The people of Israel followed Joshua across the Jordan River and learned to pull together and wage warfare in the might of the Lord. God finally gave them "rest from all their enemies around them" (Josh. 23:1 NIV). Jesus said to His followers, "Come to me, all you who are weary and burdened, and I will give you rest. Take my yoke upon

you and learn from me, for I am gentle and humble in heart, and you will find rest for your souls. For my yoke is easy and my burden is light" (Matt. 11:28-30 NIV). God's rest, it seems, is in a category of its own, in that the enemies may still await us, but we are protected from their onslaught. As we trade our yoke for His, we have the possibility of experiencing even that fleeting rest in the midst of warfare as a place of safety. And I have wondered, as some of the precious saints of

God have faced their own deaths, if they don't feel most of all like the climbers who have persisted through the trees and who can now stretch out and rest in the sunshine with a truly glorious view spread out before them. They have come into the rest for which all of us long and strain.

- *Linda Joiner*

My dear and loving Father, I praise You that You provide a pure rest, even in the midst of the battles of my life. Father, help me to look to You, in any and every situation, and to trust that You will keep my feet from stumbling. Oh, Lord, You have been good to me. Amen.

The Harbor of Peace

And let the peace of God
rule in your hearts, to which
also you were called in one
body; and be thankful.

Colossians 3:15 (NKJV)

"And in His will is our peace," wrote Dante. Intuitively we know this. When we are grounded in God's will, we are at peace. We have no reason for unrest because we are where we are supposed to be.

An interesting study of children reveals something uncanny about us as humans. Imagine two playgrounds that have identical play equipment: the same swings, slides, monkey bars, ropes, and games. They have the same amount of space around them and the same kind of wood chips on the ground. Only one feature distinguishes the first from the second: The first has a simple chain-link fence surrounding it, and the second has no fence at all, only open space.

The same number of children begin to play on each playground. Delighted at first, they play together, and then an unusual change sets in. The group on the fenced playground continues to play happily, running freely around the entire area of the playground, right up to the fence. The group on the second playground hovers around the playset, not venturing far. Timid, they play a little but don't have nearly the same amount of fun and freedom that the other children have. The children who are fenced in know their boundaries. They feel a sense of safety because of a simple fence. Without that structure, the children can't play to their hearts' content.

We're much the same way. By giving us His Word, God encloses our playground with a fence. He does it to free us. Within His will, we can run, play, grow, and delight in what He has given us. Outside of His will we act timid, ashamed, and unfulfilled. Happy obedience brings a great sense of peace.

Although we tend to value such qualities as freedom, self-determination, and leadership, we often miss the peace found in following Someone who knows our needs. When we try to assert our wills with God, we imperil the peace of our souls.

God calls us to something different. He calls us to obedience, to submission, and to servanthood. With obedience come blessings; the submissive follower of God knows the peace of God. During those times when we elevate our own selfish ambitions, making decisions on our own without submitting to the lordship of our heavenly Father, we forfeit the grace that would be ours. When the self eclipses the Savior, darkness follows. The path defined by self is a dark and lonely one, and he who walks it finds that it ends in resentment.

So God provides another way, the path of obedience. Obedience to Christ has a startling effect: It frees you. Contrary to the fear of losing your identity or being confined by harsh rules, following the plans of Christ sets you free to live life to the fullest. Obedience is the harbor of peace, the place of still waters in the midst of life.

- Paige Drygas

My Father God, I pray that I will center my life in Your will. Help me to submit my heart to You, to trust that You know what is best for me, and to follow Your will, not mine. I know that true freedom and peace are found only in You, and I pray for Your peace to rule in my heart. Like the peaceful eye of the storm, Your will is my refuge in the storms of life. Amen.

Rooted in Christ

Though the fig tree
may not blossom,
Nor fruit be on the vines;
Though the labor of the
olive may fail,
And the fields yield no food;
Though the flock be cut off
from the fold,
And there be no herd
in the stalls—
Yet I will rejoice
in the LORD,
I will joy in the God
of my salvation.
The LORD God
is my strength;
He will make my feet
like deer's feet,
And He will make me
walk on my high hills.

Habakkuk 3:17–19 (KJV)

Peace is oftentimes associated with the worst of times in someone's life. Very often, as a child of God cries out in despair for help, even then God grants a sense of inner peace. Though He does not always still the storm of trouble, He will guard the Christian's heart.

When everything seems to be going well in life—the strong marriage, the quick promotion, the children's success, the wise investments—we may be lulled into a false sense of peace. But the absence of trouble is not what defines peace. Peace is not some cheap commodity, nor is it a magic spell to cast when problems arise. Peace is not a fragile balance that tips with the slightest disturbance. If peace were that delicate, it could not carry us through trials. It would disappoint us at every turn.

Consider what the psalmist meant when he wrote, "Whom have I in heaven but You? And there is none upon earth that I desire besides You. My flesh and my heart fail; But God is the strength of my heart and my portion forever" (Ps. 73:25–26 NKJV). Though everything may collapse around me, my marriage may disintegrate, my child may fall away, my investment portfolio may crash, my career may be leveled— even then when my flesh is weakest and my heart is wrenched with pain— I have You. You are my portion forever.

Do you believe that God is enough? If He were the only thing that you had, could you be satisfied? Therein lies the secret to true peace. If your peace depends on your circumstances or upon other people, you have no peace. If your peace is linked to a spouse or friend, that person will inevitably fail you, and your façade of

peace will crumble. If your peace is linked to success, you will fail, and your peace will fall apart. Thoughtfully consider your peace. To whom or to what is it linked? If it is bound in Christ, you will stand. If not, you will fall.

When you desperately need the peace of Christ, pray earnestly for it. The Father who gives good gifts to His precious children will breathe into you the fresh wind of the Spirit. The Spirit will bear fruit in your life, blossoming rich peace. It does not come from you. It is not linked to you. It is a gift to you from your Father, which is why you can bear peace even in the darkest hour.

And thus we can affirm with the writer of Habakkuk that though the tree does not blossom, the crops fail, and the labor is in vain, yet even then I will hope in the Lord. I will joy, deliberately and wholeheartedly, in the God of my salvation, who is my strength.

- *Paige Drygas*

My loving Jesus, I come to You alone for my peace. Please help me to discern those times when I try to rely on anyone or anything else, and forgive me. Thank You that I can trust in You as my portion forever, though everything else may fall away. Thank You that You will never fail me. In Your strength I will find my peace. Amen.

Fulfillment

Peace I leave with you,
My peace I give to you;
not as the world gives do
I give to you. Let not your
heart be troubled, neither
let it be afraid.

John 14:27 (NKJV)

"*A musician must make*
music, an artist must paint,
a poet must write, if he is
to be ultimately at peace
with himself. What a
man can be, he must be."

Abraham Harold Maslow

You. From the moment of your conception, you have been known. The Lord has searched you, and He knows you (Psalm 139). He knows where you walk, what you think, when you fear, who you are. When He looks at you, He sees beyond who you are at this very second to who you can become. And He intends to complete you, His masterpiece, in all your brilliance. For when He looks at you, He does not just see the layers of despair and failure, the wrinkles worn from sin and pain, the resignation of a tired spirit. He sees beyond that.

Thank goodness He doesn't disregard us because we're incomplete. He infused each of us with character, meaning, and experiences with a certain end result in mind. A potter does not begin to mold the clay without a vision in mind. So too, God has a claim on your life, and if you will become the person He intended, you will find fulfillment.

Each of us is gifted with specific talents. Highly visible, profitable, envied talents are worth no more than simple, humble, anonymous gifts. To God, the issue is whether or not you fulfill your potential, not how your potential compares to another's. While one person is gifted to speak, another is gifted to serve. One may have a heart for orphan children, another a passion for the dying. An inspired person can radically unleash the passion of God.

And in becoming who you are compelled to be, you will find peace. The apostle Paul faced constant danger during his ministry yet expressed serene contentment. He knew that he had become the person whom God intended, and he was doing the good work that God had for him. Queen Esther knew the same peace, even under threat of death. Believing that she had come to power "for such a time as this," she stepped boldly into the role that God had for her. May you discover that same surprising peace. To suppress your God-given talents will disappoint you. Whatever you were meant to do, do it—with all your heart and for his glory.

- *Paige Drygas*

Lord of my life, I pray that You will help me to become all that You intended. I trust that You see the potential in me and that You can use me for Your glory. Flood me with a sense of purpose and grant me the peace that comes from living in You. In Your gracious name I pray Amen.

Thomas
Kinkade

From Strength to Strength

*Blessed are those whose
strength is in you,
who have set their hearts on
pilgrimage . . .
They go from strength to
strength,
till each appears before God
in Zion.*

Psalm 84:5, 7 (NIV)

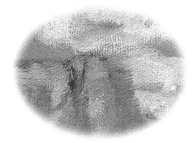

Pilgrimage . . . the word implies a journey, long-distance travel, challenges, and a hope and longing for home. When we rely on God for our strength, we naturally set our hearts on a pilgrimage to heaven. Though we live in this world, our hearts belong in the next—not in an impractical way of ignoring life, but in a wise realization that life extends beyond time, gravity, the sky, paychecks, and physical pain. When Paul suggested in Colossians 3:2, that we set our minds on things above, not on earthly things, he did not imply that we take a mental vacation but rather that we put our hope in something secure that will never disappoint us. And so our hearts belong in heaven.

This is what God intended for us in Christ. We billow along from strength to strength, resting in His secure places, until we appear before Him in Zion. As pilgrims, we know that our real home is in and with Christ Jesus, our King. Until we join Him forever, we can rest with Him in prayer and journey from strength to strength. The words of Charles Wesley's hymn "Soldiers of Christ, Arise" capture the spirit of trust with which we can approach our trustworthy Savior.

From strength to strength go on,
wrestle and fight and pray,
tread all the powers of darkness down
and win the well-fought day.
Still let the Spirit cry
in all his soldiers, "Come!"
till Christ the Lord, descends from high
and takes the conquerors home.

In one of the last lines of the hymn, Wesley encourages believers, "From strength to strength go on." His words echo the psalmist's, who wrote of the blessed pilgrim who goes from strength to strength until he appears before God in heaven.

Until that glorious day, we must rely on His strengths. And how, we wonder, might those strengths manifest themselves? He gives us His strengths in compelling ways:

- Through His Word. Our daily sustenance, to feed us and nourish our spirits. In the Bible, we find pertinent words of encouragement to direct our paths.
- Through prayer. Time spent with God in prayer is time of comfort and peace. Through prayer, the Spirit ministers to our deepest needs.
- Through other believers. God uses our brothers and sisters in Christ to build us up. As the body of Christ, we can encourage each other with the audible words and visible sympathy that we crave.
- Through the Spirit. Within us lives and moves a Spirit that we can neither define nor control. His mysterious work within us knows no bounds.

- Paige Drygas

Sweet Jesus, I thank You that You will carry me from strength to strength. Help me to trust that You know when I need to rest and that You will provide the strength I need to continue in this pilgrimage. For all Your goodness, I give You thanks, and I pray for the peace that comes from relying on Your strength. Amen.

Home at Last

❦

Through many dangers,
toils, and snares,
I have already come;
'Tis grace has brought me
safe thus far,
and grace will lead
me home.
From "Amazing Grace"
John Newton (1725–1807)

Home—in the sense of a resting place, the journey's end, a place to be and to abide—is a deeply felt human conception, a universal longing. If you've ever spent time around horses, either trail horses for recreational riding or workhorses on a ranch or farm, you've seen the strength of that longing expressed even by animals. Regardless of how long the journey, they are capable of finding renewed energy when they sense that they're close to home. "Hold 'er, Newt—she's headed for the barn!" is a favorite cowboy adage repeated by more than one tourist wrangler. That longing for the familiar place where food, water, and shelter await, where the burden of saddle and bridle are shed, is something that humans—from commuters to manual laborers—can identify with. In addition, home is the focus of all our work and striving, the place we mean to build up, to establish, and to protect so that we may enjoy it indefinitely.

This concept runs throughout God's revelation to humankind. Inextricably woven into God's command for Abram to abandon one home ("Leave your country, your people and your father's household and go to the land I will show you") was His promise to provide another, better home. And this quest became the guiding principle of the people of Israel for generations afterward. Home. Where we belong. Where we rest, establish our lineage, and prosper. Where enemies are securely held at bay. Where the worship of God is foundational to our lives. All this is what God promised to His people if they, like Abram, would obey.

Of course, in subsequent days, sometimes Abraham obeyed, and sometimes he did not. Sometimes his children and their children and their children let God define home for them, and sometimes they did not. The cry of the exiles, recorded in Psalm 137, is plaintive proof of how deeply the sense of home had become established in their hearts: "By the rivers of Babylon we sat and wept when we remembered Zion" (Ps. 137:1 NIV).

For Christians, all of these are but illustrations of a spiritual reality. The majority of North Americans may not resonate with the urge to move toward home, due to our incredible degree of physical comfort. But the truth remains that nowhere in this world is truly home. Hebrews 13:14 says, "For here we do not have an enduring city, but we are looking for the city that is to come" (NIV). We have more in common with the exile and the refugee. As we journey toward home, we store up treasure. Jesus said, "Do not store up for yourselves treasures on earth, where moth and rust destroy, and where thieves break in and steal. But store up for yourselves treasures in heaven, where moth and rust do not destroy, and where thieves do not break in and steal. For where your treasure is, there your heart will be also" (Matt. 6:19–21 NIV). To this end, we strain and long.

- *Linda Joiner*

My loving God, thank You for instilling a sense of home within me. May I set my heart evermore on my one true home, which is with You. Please direct my steps along the journey, that I may store up my eternal treasure securely with You. Amen.

An Image of Peace

Don't worry about any-
thing; instead, pray about
everything. Tell God what
you need, and thank him for
all he has done. If you do
this, you will experience
God's peace, which is far
more wonderful than the
human mind can under-
stand. His peace will guard
your hearts and minds as
you live in Christ Jesus.

Philippians 4:6–7 (NLT)

What is your image of peace? Do you picture a world without conflicts between nations and groups of people? Do you think of a state of mind that exists when you are in a special place, enjoying the beauty of God's nature, far removed from the stress of daily life? Do you imagine peace to be a good feeling resulting from a harmonious relationship, or an attitude that you can achieve by eliminating negative thoughts and by thinking positively?

Our culture embraces these ideals as peace. We talk about world peace, where people live in harmony with one another and where war and strife no longer exist. Inner peace results from an individual's state of mind, when negative thoughts are systematically removed and replaced with positive ones. We seek to be "at peace" and "one" with our surroundings and nature. Reality paints a much starker picture. War and hatred because of skin color and religion rage throughout our world. Inner peace is often usurped by self-doubt, depression, and anxiety. Tornadoes, floods, and other natural disasters rip apart those tranquil, scenic vistas.

So where can you find a clearer image of peace? For the Christian, true peace does not come from good feelings, positive thinking, scenes of nature, or absence of war. Peace comes from knowing that God is in control. It comes from knowing that our final destination is not earth, but heaven, and that our story is

not finalized at death, but is just beginning. It comes from knowing that we have a Savior who has given us victory over the sin that causes us despair.

When I first became a Christian in my adult years, I clung to these verses from Philippians. I cherished the image of God's peace wrapping itself around my mind and my heart, guarding me against self-doubt, anxious thoughts, nagging worries, and relentless fears. I still do. With that image of peace, it doesn't matter where I am, what my circumstances are, or what is happening in today's headlines. God's peace is always available, always protecting, always guarding me in His love and provision.

- *Betsy Schmitt*

Thank You, Lord, for Your peace. Thank You that you give us a peace that does not depend on our feelings, our circumstances, or our surroundings. Thank You that Your peace is solely dependent on who You are and on Your promises that are found in Christ Jesus, Your Son. Thank You for Your peace that protects and guards us in all things. Amen.

The Stream of Life

Then the angel showed me
the river of the water of
life, as clear as crystal,
flowing from the throne of
God and of the Lamb
down the middle of the
great street of the city. On
each side of the river stood
the tree of life, bearing
twelve crops of fruit,
yielding its fruit every
month. And the leaves of
the tree are for the healing
of the nations.

Revelation 22:1–2 (NIV)

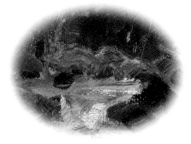

There is an apparent contradiction shown by the waters of a mountain stream as it rushes down from the melting snow of the craggy mountaintops, over the rocks and under the logs, gurgling with constant melody. The stream shows at once both a picture of ceaseless activity and of perfect rest. How can this be?

There is nothing so soothing as being lulled to sleep by the sound of a running stream. It is the ultimate, natural "white noise" when heard from your streamside tent or cabin. My mother used to break into a rendition of a piece by Mozart whenever she spotted such a stream. The music is lilting, playful, and crystalline in its beauty. The clear, pure water dances happily as occasional rocks cause it to leap skyward before plunging downward again.

The stream is an appropriate image for the perpetual motion of our lives. Its flow is relentless, day and night. Its activity creates a roar that can be heard from far away. To temporarily dam its flow requires constant vigilance, as the beaver well knows. Its rush will eventually break through the most carefully constructed barrier. Our lives, too, tend to swirl with busyness as we rush from one urgent call to the next. Because some of the urgency is important and some is not, our sense of purpose and our energy become drained. At the end of a day, the myriad of worries creates a restless drone in our sleep, rather than a lullaby.

Lilt or roar? Soothing or frantic? In part, our life experience is determined by a habit or discipline of the Christian life, which is also best exemplified by a

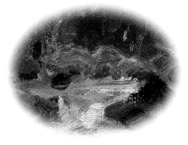

bubbling stream. In 1 Thessalonians 5:16–18, Paul exhorted us: "Be joyful always; pray continually; give thanks in all circumstances, for this is God's will for you in Christ Jesus" (NIV). Prayer is more than our deliberate drawing aside to speak to God, important as that is. Continual prayer is much like the activity of that rushing stream. It leaps with joy, it bathes the difficulties of our lives and the tragedies of our world in tears, it infuses our very being with strength and energy, and it never ceases.

Perhaps this way of being is also what Paul alluded to in Ephesians 5 when he said, "Live as children of light" (5:8 NIV). In verses 18-20, he elaborated: "Be filled with the Spirit. Speak to one another with psalms, hymns and spiritual songs. Sing and make music in your heart to the Lord, always giving thanks to God the Father for everything, in the name of our Lord Jesus Christ" (NIV). The most important "activity" of the Christian is really the current of the Holy Spirit flowing through our lives. In this way, may we grow to be like the bubbling mountain stream. Amen.

- *Linda Joiner*

Gracious Lord, please fill me fresh with the Holy Spirit. I pray that His work in me may trickle down into my mind and heart, and may He well up within me as a vibrant, dancing stream. Though my life is filled with distractions, help me to be marked by continual prayer and communion with You. Amen.

Glimpses into His Sanctuary

O God, you are my God,

earnestly I seek you;

my soul thirsts for you,

my body longs for you,

in a dry and weary land

where there is no water.

I have seen you in the

sanctuary and beheld your

power and your glory.

Because your love is better

than life, my lips will glorify

you. I will praise you as

long as I live, and in your

name I will lift up

my hands.

Psalm 63:1–4 (NIV)

Some of my greatest experiences of exhilaration and accomplishment have happened in the mountains. Particularly in places where the heights rise above timberline, it is possible, with exertion and effort, to reach a point where an incredible vista opens before you. From a rocky crag or a pass between two valleys, you may be able to see for a hundred miles in any direction. Other mountains and other valleys fill the foreground. Distant plains are visible beyond. Human settlements are dwarfed by the geological landmarks.

If you watch for a while at your lofty vantage point, you may very well see clouds swirling up one valley or down another, followed by glorious streaks as the rain is highlighted by sunshine beyond. To see the weather so brilliantly is a rich reward for those who climb. But it also constitutes one of the primary dangers. Afternoon thunderstorms are common in the mountains. They often bathe one valley yet leave another dry. To be on the heights when the clouds move overhead is foolish. The lightning seeks the highest point, which in the absence of trees may very well be the climber.

The perspective from a mountain overlook may be likened to moments of spiritual insight and awe. Suddenly we can view our lives as if from above, and we gain an understanding of God's loving purpose in an emotional landscape that has

seemed without rhyme or reason. But in our human frailty, we cannot stay there forever. We are not equipped to live at those heights. Those moments are gifts that encourage us to trust in the God who created it all and continues to oversee it all. The "mountaintop" experiences are the closest thing we will know in this life to the sanctuary of God. With that great encouragement in our hearts, we can affirm these words along with the hymn writer. Make this thought your prayer of praise today.

- *Linda Joiner*

God is working his purpose out as year succeeds to year: God is working his purpose out, and the time is drawing near; Nearer and nearer draws the time, the time that shall surely be, when the earth shall be filled with the glory of God as the waters cover the sea. Arthur Campbell Ainger (1841–1919)

The Unchanging Rock

My soul finds rest
in God alone;
my salvation
comes from him.
He alone is my rock
and my salvation;
he is my fortress,
I will never be shaken.

Psalm 62:1–2 (NIV)

A mountain like Mount Ranier, massive and rocky, majestic in its solidity, is an apt meditation upon God's might and changelessness. Staring up at its craggy top reminds us of our own insignificance and frailty. Imagine climbing over those enormous boulders, up those sheer rock faces. What incredible forces must have shaped it! Yet it remains unmoved through all the changes of season and weather.

Many a mountain watcher has delightedly photographed the same specific peak again and again, noting how cloud and shadow, bright sun and blowing snow can change the scene. But the mountain itself remains recognizable by the outlines of its shoulders, the unique profile of its rock faces. It is and always will be Mount Ranier. How much more is our God unchanged by the winds of history and the whims of human thought! Paul stated emphatically, "Jesus Christ is the same yesterday and today and forever" (Heb. 13:8 NIV).

It has been said that change is the only "given" in our modern world. In one sense, this thought is invigorating and inspiring. The frontiers of scientific understanding and of medicine are constantly changing, enabling humankind, at least theoretically, to better the span and quality of our lives. New inventions, or faster, more efficient versions of old ones, appear with great regularity. Yet the universality and constancy of change can also be unsettling. Can our minds keep pace with the changes around us? And what of our need for stability? For principles and persons we can count on? For a firm soil in which to be rooted and grounded? In this sense, the modern world has little to offer. Just as God

Himself was the central premise for the psalmists, giving meaning to their existence and to the world around them, so God is for us today. He has not changed. To be human is to find our meaning as His creatures—beloved, fallen, but redeemed. "In him we live and move and have our being" (Acts 17:28 NIV). Though everything may change around us—these central truths do not.

Thus we can have hope in a world that too often seems bereft of hope. Even the image of the "changeless" mountain peak is inadequate to express the greater truth of God's immutability. Psalm 46 says, "God is our refuge and strength, an ever-present help in trouble. Therefore we will not fear, though the earth give way and the mountains fall into the heart of the sea, though its waters roar and foam and the mountains quake with their surging" (Ps. 46:1–3 NIV). Those who witnessed the news photographs of the eruption of Mount Saint Helens can well imagine the catastrophic transformation of a seemingly solid mountain. Our God is exponentially greater, more dependable, more constant. We need not hesitate to put our trust in Him.

- *Linda Joiner*

My unchanging Rock, how great is Your faithfulness. You are constant, unshakable, and true. Thank You for being the source of my stability and the foundation on which I can stand. I praise You, my Father, for being the rock of my hope. Amen.

Stillness

*Be still, and know
that I am God;
I will be exalted
among the nations,
I will be exalted
in the earth!*

Psalm 46:10 (NKJV)

As the Supreme Artist, God creates what humans can only recreate. The breathtaking scene brushed on a canvas is but a limited reflection of the majesty God first orchestrated in nature. The artist's paint pales next to God's rich hues. Majestic scenes of nature bear the unmistakable signature of the Creator.

When you behold such natural beauty—the glow of a golden sunset, the glassy water of a still lake, the majesty of the mountains rising above you—listen for His voice, bringing you soothing words to focus your mind on one thing. "Be still, and know that I am God." The speed of everyday life may often leave you feeling overwhelmed. How can you balance all of the forces that compete for your attention, let alone set aside time for quiet reflection? And God simply says, "Be still."

Like an antsy child who can't sit still, I fidget and squirm before my heavenly Father. My eyes shift and wander. Slowly I wind down, casting aside my preoccupations, and I find what I had been missing all along.

"Where there is peace and meditation, there is neither anxiety nor doubt," wrote St. Francis of Assisi. In those rare, still moments of communion with the Father, peace reigns. Anxiety and doubt cannot plague you when you have cleared your mind of worry to meditate on your God.

In our stillness, He asks us to fill our minds with just one thought: "Know that I am God." To know that He is God is to acknowledge Him as the Lord of all. He is not just the Lord of Sundays or religion. He can't be confined; He won't be dismissed. He is the Lord of every day, of every thought, of every discipline. He is the Lord of good times and bad, of medicine, of economics, of art, of joy and disappointment. For on the final day, every knee will bow, yours and mine, and together we will confess that Jesus Christ is Lord. We can release everything to His lordship, letting go of what overwhelms us. In our stillness we find peace.

- *Paige Drygas*

Lord, so often I am distracted by the activities in my life, and I allow myself to be swept up with anxiety. Teach me to be still. Fill my mind with thoughts of You, for You alone are Lord of all. Apart from You there is no good thing. You are all I need, and I find rest in You. Amen.

Forgiveness

"I tell you, her sins—and they are many—have been forgiven, so she has shown me much love. But a person who is forgiven little shows only little love." Then Jesus said to the woman, "Your sins are forgiven. . . . Your faith has saved you; go in peace."

Luke 7:47–50 (NLT)

Perhaps the heart that truly knows peace is the one that holds nothing left to forgive, nothing unforgiven. Resentment and guilt corrode peace like bitter acid, eating away at the tender flesh of the heart, diminishing it to cold stone.

Forgiveness is a cleansing well. As we draw from it, we drink of the cool water of forgiveness for our sins, and then we must share the saving waters with those who need our forgiveness. The first always precedes the second. Before we can forgive others their sins against us, we must first ask our heavenly Father to forgive our sins. He never refuses. He floods us with grace and forgiveness, and out of that bottomless well of forgiveness, we can draw the grace to forgive others.

When tragedy hits us, friends deceive us, spouses disappoint us, or loved ones betray us, pain forces a decision. The pain of loss and betrayal can be so sharp that it destroys us. Each of us must decide, Will I be able to forgive them, though they never ask it and do not deserve it? Or will I grow colder each day, calloused with anger, silently dying inside?

Our opportunities to forgive can be some of the toughest battles we fight. Only God can perfectly forgive, but if we don't try, we can never have peace. In those dark times, we can turn to Jesus and ask Him to teach us to forgive, to enable us to forgive, and most of all—to help us realize the amount that we

have been forgiven. As terrible as the sins committed against us, they pale in comparison to the gross offenses we have committed against our loving Father. We forgive because He first forgave us. A heart at peace has learned how to forgive.

What unresolved conflict comes to mind when you think about forgiveness? What broken relationship needs to be healed? The slow work of resentment is to petrify the soul. By taking the initiative to restore, mend, and heal, we cleanse our own hearts with the waters of forgiveness.

- Paige Drygas

Father, I come to You humbly to ask for Your forgiveness. I am an imperfect, broken person, and I have failed You. I thank You for graciously forgiving and cleansing me, and I ask that You will help me to forgive others. Lord, soften my heart toward those who have hurt me, and give me the grace to forgive them as You have forgiven me. Thank you for the peace that comes through forgiveness. Amen.

Peace Among the Rocks

Come to Me, all you who
labor and are heavy laden,
and I will give you rest.
Take My yoke upon you
and learn from Me, for I
am gentle and lowly in heart,
and you will find rest for
your souls. For My yoke is
easy and My burden is light.
Matthew 11:28–30 (NKJV)

If Jesus had been born into a palace instead of a manger, would He be able to relate to you? If He had come down in glory, escorted by angels, would He know what it was like to be you? If He had never faced temptation, nor known the pangs of hunger, nor felt the pain of loss, would He be a compassionate Savior? What does it mean to us that His feet got dusty from walking, that He cried at the tomb of His friend Lazarus, that He was rejected by His closest friends, and that He felt such anxiety that He sweat drops of blood?

It says something about Him, doesn't it? Though He could have chosen an easier way, He opted for a full human life and an excruciating death. He experienced every emotion, joy, disappointment, pain, and exhaustion. Because of the way He lived His life, He has something to offer us that He would not otherwise have: comfort. He can empathize with you. When you face your lowest times, weighed down with depression and burdens, He knows your pain. The Savior who loved you enough to live and die for you can also relate to you.

Thus Jesus can offer us comfort. His invitation shows humility and strength. "Come to Me," He invites, "and I will carry your burden. I will give you a light load, and I will give you rest." Those words of comfort ring with truth because He lived as one of us.

"Even among these rocks, our peace is His will," wrote the Christian literary scholar T. S. Eliot. When your life crashes against the rocks, even then He wants to give you peace. Often we associate peace with idyllic seasons of life, when absolutely nothing could go wrong. But if we can have peace only when our lives are "perfect," will we ever have peace? Our peace cannot be tied to our circumstances; it must have a deeper source. Through Christ, we can have peace even when the car is wrecked, the taxes are late, the business folds, the family is torn, the friendship disintegrates, and joy seems distant. Even among these rocks, He can give us peace.

His is not a glib offer. He does not suggest that we fake our smiles or pretend that our lives are not falling apart. Sometimes we just cannot smile and our circumstances seem unbearable for a long time. But even during the worst of times, we can know the peace of Christ that surpasses our understanding. When we cry out for His help and cast our cares on Him, He will surprise us with peace, little by little. With His peace, we can withstand the storm.

- *Paige Drygas*

Lord Jesus, thank You for living a human life so that You understand my weaknesses. Thank You for being a compassionate Savior. Help me to cast my burdens on You; please take them from me. I pray for a lighter load and for the peace that is found only in You. In Your precious name, Amen.

Notice His Presence

The LORD bless you
and keep you;
the LORD make his face
shine upon you
and be gracious to you;
the LORD turn his face
toward you
and give you peace.

Numbers 6:24–26 (NIV)

Your panic is terrifying. As a six-year-old, you reach up into the crowd of bodies to take your daddy's hand. But the hand you grab is not your daddy's. You snatch it back. The man smiles kindly at you, but you don't want him. You want your own daddy. You had become so interested in the antics of the chimpanzees at the zoo that you didn't hear your dad say, "Come on, let's go see the orangutans. They're even funnier."

Now as the crowd presses against you, eager to see the shenanigans you have been watching, you see no one you recognize, nothing familiar. What will you do? Where will you go? Who will help you?

The little girl next to you has her mommy's hand firmly in her own. The boy on the other side of the cage has his daddy kneeling beside him. But where is your daddy?

You call his name.

No answer.

You push through the crowd.

Only an unending sea of legs with unfamiliar shoes.

Then you feel the warm, reassuring touch of a hand on your shoulder. It's your daddy. Your very own daddy. Realizing that you were missing, he quickly came back for you. As immediately as panic seized you, peace now floods you.

Daddy is close by, and despite the throng of activity around you, everything is OK. The two of you head for the orangutans together.

Peace is not always quiet; it's not the same as stillness. Peace is the presence of your Father, your very own God, in the midst of the hubbub. While you drive those endless five miles to pick up your very ill child at school, God is with you, assuring you that He will show you how to make her comfortable. As the faces of lying coworkers haunt you in the wee hours of the morning, God is there to comfort you back to sleep. Peace can be had during times of great happiness or right in the middle of heart-bursting agony. Why? Because it is a gift that God gives you, His resource for handling the madness.

Just as a small child would do, reach out to embrace the peace that God offers you. Let it wash over you, empowering you and equipping you for what is at hand.

- *Karen Dockery*

My dear and gracious Father, please bless and keep me. Thank You for shining Your face upon me and for being gracious to me. Please turn Your face toward me, and show me how to accept Your peace. Amen.

Choose Peace

❦

Salt is good, but if it loses its saltiness, how can you make it salty again? Have salt in yourselves, and be at peace with each other.

Mark 9:50 (NIV)

Sometimes God gives peace through external circumstances. Imagine that you are sitting in your backyard, watching your baby splash in the wading pool. His absolute delight at the simple pleasure of slapping the magical water fills you with joy. You let that maple-syrup warmness spill over and wash your whole being. This peace that surpasses understanding is an unmistakable gift from God through your tiny son.

But you have to choose it.

You can just as easily grow aggravated that his splashing ruins the magazine page you're reading. Or that he won't play with the expensive pool toy you just purchased.

You might argue, "I would never do that! Everyone knows that life's simple pleasures are the best and that a baby's delight is much more important than a magazine." But whining is a powerful enemy, bent on consuming your peace and stealing away from you the smidgens of peace that God presents to you in unsuspecting moments.

So watch out.

And watch above.

There you will find power stronger than any complaint or groaning. There you will find the resolve to choose peace. "Be at peace with each other"

(Mark 9:50 NIV) is a call to action. Choosing peace is a decision, not something you wait to feel.

And you can feast on that action with absolute abandon. Consider joining in the splash-fest with your baby. Delight in the steady cooperation you and your coworkers share. Embrace the 437 questions your four-year-old asks every day, a certain sign that she's eager to learn about God's very good world. Simple action by simple action, choose a habit of peace.

- Karen Dockery

God, remind me not to save up peace for a bigger moment, a tougher time, a happier encounter. Teach me the joy of savoring the bits of peace You poke into the most hectic of days. Help me to model peace for my family, my coworkers, and my church family. Thank You for Your unending supply; help me to drink thirstily. Amen.

Thomas
Kinkade

God's Wonderful Creation

*Then God saw everything
that He had made, and
indeed it was very good . . .
Thus the heavens and the
earth, and all the host of
them, were finished. And on
the seventh day God ended
His work which He had
done, and He rested on the
seventh day from all His
work which He had done.*

Genesis 1:31—2:2 (NKJV)

The soft, tropical breeze rippled the surface of the ocean and then played among the fronds of the coconut palms. The playful breeze carried along heady perfumes from the gorgeous flowers. Strange, exotic birdcalls mixed with the crashing surf and the rhythms of an island melody. I absorbed all of these warm, tropical sensations as I lay under an umbrella on a Hawaiian beach on the island of Kauai.

"Think we could just be beach bums and stay here forever?" I asked my husband.

"Sure," he said. "We could sell seashells by the seashore, eat coconuts, and sleep under the palm trees."

It sounded tempting. Kauai was a whole different world from anywhere we had ever been. It seemed like the closest thing to the perfect world God created. Island life moved at a much slower pace than it did in Chicago, and the people had plenty of time for each other. As the days passed, I could feel myself releasing the tensions, stresses, and worries I often carry around—sort of like a snake shedding its skin. For once, I felt fully relaxed, taking time to enjoy talking with my husband, walking on the beach, and enjoying God's beautiful creation.

Not surprisingly, we did not become beach bums, and we returned to untropical Chicago. But, even eight years later, a part of that trip stays with me. I can recall those lovely sensations. And as I remember Kauai, I smile and relax.

In God's world, everything He made was very good. He made it for us to enjoy. We don't need to travel to Hawaii or some other faraway place to enjoy nature. The beauty and wonder of it are all around us—on farms, in the mountains or deserts, in city parks, and by the seashore. But it's difficult to enjoy and appreciate the beauty of God's creation when we rush through our days, hurrying from one thing or place to another. We need to slow down, to relax, and to really look at all the marvelous things God made.

Following God's example, we are to "rest from all the work we do." If God is so almighty that He can just speak the whole universe into existence, then why does He need to rest? God did not rest because He was tired. An all-powerful God doesn't need to rest. God modeled a pattern that He wanted His people to follow.

Our world is action-oriented. God demonstrated that rest is right and appropriate. If God took time off and rested from His work of creation, then it should not amaze us that we need rest as well. Our times of rest give us peace and refresh us to serve God.

Take some time each day to rest and soak it all in—or listen to the birds or watch snowflakes fall or praise Him for His wonderful creation.
- *Jeanette Dall*

Creator God, thank You for creating a world full of beauty and wonder. Teach me to take the time to rest and enjoy my life in this world. Help me to know the relaxation and contentment that comes from simply being. Amen.

Thomas
Kinkade

Renewing Rain

There remains therefore a
rest for the people of God.
For he who has entered His
rest has himself also ceased
from his works as God did
from His.

Hebrews 4:9-10 (NKJV)

Imagine yourself in the middle of an extended heat wave during the dog days of summer. The temperature rises into the nineties, the sky is cloudless, and the sun blazes, sucking up every drop of moisture. The grass turns brown, flowers wilt, and cars overheat. Going outside is like walking into the blast of a furnace—you can now identify with Shadrach, Meshach, and Abednego.

You try to keep things alive by running the sprinkler, but it doesn't help very much. And then, in the middle of the night, you hear the sound of a gentle rain. You hope that it will keep raining for a whole day—and it does! The ground soaks up the water like a sponge, and people don't mind driving or walking in the rain. This rain renews, bringing new life to the crops in the fields, the grass in the lawns, and the tomatoes and flowers in home gardens. It washes the city streets and brings a freshness to everything. The rain is restful and relaxing—it gives a sense of peace to people as they watch things turn green right before their eyes.

Our lives sometimes feel like a summer heat wave. We get hot and bothered about things in our home life and our work. We nearly dry up and wilt under all the things that beat us down. We try to take care of things ourselves, but things just don't work out. But, God and His Word are like a renewing summer shower. As Paul writes in Hebrews 4:9, "There remains therefore a rest for the people of God."

What is God's rest? For Christians, it is peace with God now and eternal life in heaven later. We do not need to wait until heaven to enjoy God's rest and peace; we may have it every day, right now! Our rest in Christ begins when we trust God to do His good and perfect work in and through us. When we believe in Christ as our Savior, we enter this place of rest, which is peace with God and enjoyment of His spiritual blessing. Our daily rest in God doesn't end with death but becomes even more wonderful in the eternal home Jesus is preparing for us.

When the believer enters God's rest, it is a "ceasing from his works." We stop relying on what we do and trust securely in what Christ has done on the cross. We find rest from trying to earn salvation and blessings for ourselves. Jesus did it all.

The next time it rains, remember how we are showered with God's gracious love and blessings. And then go out and splash in a few puddles!

- Jeanette Dall

God of rest, thank You for the renewing rains that You send to the dry earth. Help me to enjoy these showers and to remember that they are one of Your physical blessings. Thank You for the spiritual blessings that You shower on me every day, for forgiveness and eternal life. Help me to enjoy Your rest now and forever in heaven. Amen.

Thorny Beauty

❧

Blessed are they

whose transgressions

are forgiven,

whose sins are covered.

Romans 4:7 (NIV)

The most beloved and well-recognized flower is the rose. Roses come in a multitude of colors, sizes, and varieties. Walking through a large garden like the Rose Garden in Portland surrounds you with powerful scents. The velvety petals, beautiful colors, and heady aroma invite you to come closer and even to lean down and inhale. But be careful! The most beautiful roses also have the sharpest thorns. It seems quite ironic that such a beautiful flower can inflict sharp pain.

The promises of the world can be likened to a rose garden. They appear in a variety of forms, all promising peace, tranquility, and serenity. Some of them direct us to an inner place of peace. Others recommend prescribed diets or lengthy periods of meditation. But be careful! These worldly promises can cause more hurt than a bloody finger.

The peace the world promises is usually an absence of conflict with oneself or those around us. It is a psychological state of mind found in positive thinking or in good feelings. That kind of peace is short-lived and unsatisfactory. The peace that Jesus promises is the result of the Holy Spirit's work in our lives. It is a deep and lasting peace that is confident of God's love and care in any circumstance. With Jesus' peace, we need not fear the present or the future. This peace comes from knowing that we are forgiven through Christ. Because of Him, we have fellowship with God.

God's peace is different from the world's peace because it is real peace. Because God is in control, our victory over sin is certain. The peace of God is an inner tranquility based on peace with God—the peaceful state of those whose sins are forgiven. It is the tranquillity that comes when the believer commits all personal cares to God in prayer and worries about them no more.

All true peace is Jesus' free gift. The world's peace can only express a longing or wish. But Jesus' peace is real and present. Accept the gift and enjoy true peace—a peace without any thorns.

- Jeanette Dall

Dear Jesus, thank You for the promise of Your peace—the only true peace. Help us not to be taken in by the world's promises of peace but to commit all our worries, frustration, and cares to You. I accept Your free gift of peace. Amen.

Prison Escape

❧

"And so I tell you, keep on asking, and you will be given what you ask for. Keep on looking, and you will find. Keep on knocking, and the door will be opened. For everyone who asks, receives. Everyone who seeks, finds. And the door is opened to everyone who knocks."

Luke 11:9-10 (NLT)

Over Thanksgiving weekend, the whole family gathered for a big celebration. The days were a familiar mixture of remembering, playing, chatting, sleeping, and lots of eating. On Saturday afternoon, a light snow began to fall, and someone suggested that we take a ride in the country. Seven of us piled into the van, and off we went to enjoy the beautiful wintry day. We could see deer hunters in the fields and along the woods. "Look at the deer right along the road!" my nephew yelled.

Our driver overreacted, and in a heartbeat, the van lurched and slipped off the road. We became airborne and rolled several times before finally landing in the field. What began as a great country ride suddenly seemed like a battlefield, with moaning and bleeding relatives struggling to climb out of the wreckage. I could move, but my husband could not—his back had been seriously broken.

During the days, weeks, and months of my husband's hospitalization, surgery, and therapy, I prayed a lot. I prayed for his life, for successful surgery, and for a return of sensation and strength in his lower body. But even though I prayed, I was a prisoner of fear, depression, and anger. I became much more paralyzed emotionally than my husband was physically.

In its day, the prison on Alcatraz Island was considered one of the toughest prisons, impossible to escape. But Alcatraz prison is a pushover compared to the prisons we construct for ourselves—prisons of guilt, sin, shame, and fear. How can

we ever escape from them? They confine us day and night, no matter where we go or what we do. Their hold is stronger than reinforced steel bars.

Jesus alone has the key to unlock our personal prisons so that we can escape. Jesus invites us to come to Him and to give Him all the anger, sin, and pain that may imprison us. When we give everything to Jesus, we are set free—free to truly live in peace. Jesus gives us rest for our souls.

When I finally said, "OK, God, here are all my worries, fears, and anger. You can have them!" I felt free and unburdened. That doesn't mean that my husband's paralysis suddenly disappeared and everything returned to normal. It meant that I was at peace with myself and with the drastic changes in my life. I trusted God to take care of my family and to show us how to serve Him in new and deeper ways. The rest Jesus promises is peace with God, not the end of all effort.

- *Jeanette Dall*

Dear Lord Jesus, help me to escape from my personal prisons by giving all of my burdens to You. I surrender my pain, my sin, my anger, and all my cares to Your strong and loving arms. Release me, Lord, and make me whole, I pray. Amen.

A View from the Sky

❧

*Now we see but a poor
reflection as in a mirror; then
we shall see face to face.
Now I know in part; then I
shall know fully, even as I
am fully known.*

1 Corinthians 13:12 (NIV)

"Wow! Look at that!" my five-year-old son shouted. "And look down there! What is that?"

It was sort of hard to understand Rex, because his face was smashed up against the window of the plane, but I could definitely tell that he was excited. It was Rex's first plane ride, and he was mesmerized by the view out the window. His whole perspective of the world he knew had changed, and it was almost overwhelming for him.

My friend always requests an aisle seat on a plane, because she thinks it would be easier to get out in the event of a crash. Not me! I always request a window seat, not because I'm fearless but because I like to look at the scenery below. Sometimes I only see the top sides of the clouds, but on a clear day it does seem that you can see forever. I can follow a river for miles, as it winds its way through fields, under highways, and into a town or city. I can see the ribbons of roads, the closely packed buildings of cities, and the scattered farms of the countryside. No matter how many plane trips I take, I still feel like Rex on his very first trip. I'm always fascinated by the view—even the tops of clouds are different from what we see from the ground.

Once I'm back on the ground, my view is very limited, especially if I am in a crowded city. Sometimes I can't even see to the end of the block, or I can only glimpse a speck of sky between the buildings. The view of our life can be limited, too, as we focus on what's happening right now. We just can't see why we didn't

get the job we wanted so badly. We can't understand why we have to move to another state. We can't explain the sudden turns of events.

Sometimes I need to get a better perspective of my life when things don't quite go the way I think they should. I think of myself as having the ground view of my life while God has the aerial view—He can see the whole picture. God certainly knows what's happening right now, but He also knows what is going to happen tomorrow, next month, and all the years for the rest of my life. God even has things worked out for my eternal life in heaven. Now that is truly an awesome view!

Knowing that God sees the whole picture provides a sense of relief and imparts an inner peace to our lives. Sometimes I think back on things in my life that I worried about or times when I just couldn't understand. As I recall these past events and worries, I can finally see what God had in mind. I can see how those things fit into the big picture of God's plan for my life, and I can say, "Wow! Look at that!"

- *Jeanette Dall*

All-knowing God, too many times I get caught up in the immediate and take a limited view of my life—focusing on what is happening right now. Help me to trust You and to find peace, knowing that You have the fuller view. In Jesus' name I pray, Amen.

Sit a Spell

*And He said to them,
"Come aside by yourselves to
a deserted place and rest a
while." For there were many
coming and going, and they
did not even have time to
eat. So they departed to a
deserted place in the boat by
themselves.*

Mark 6:31–32 (NKJV)

If I could put myself into this painting of Union Square, I would be sitting on the bench under the palm trees. Perhaps I would have a cold drink with me, but no newspaper and no book to read. I would just be people-watching. People-watching is one of my favorite activities—sort of a game I play whenever I am in a crowded, busy place. As I watch the people come and go, I wonder where they are going. What are they thinking about as they pass my bench? Do any of them notice me and wonder what I'm doing, thinking, or feeling?

There are as many ways of moving along a crowded sidewalk as there are people. Some rush by, their heads down, leaning forward—these people seldom smile. Others sort of amble along, taking time to look in windows—they may smile if someone makes eye contact. Children are a whole different story. They giggle or sleep in strollers, hold a big hand or try to wiggle free, and some laugh and yell, while others cry and scream. Regardless of how they do it, they are all moving—coming and going.

Jesus and His disciples experienced this same kind of frenetic activity: "For there were many coming and going, and they did not even have time to eat." Does that sound like you? You have so many activities on your agenda that you don't even have time to eat or sit still. Maybe you do sit down or even lie down at night, but your mind keeps going, thinking of all the things on your "to-do" list.

Coming and going describes many of us. Some of us don't even know whether we are coming or going.

Jesus has a solution for our coming and going. He tells the disciples and us, "Come aside by yourselves to a deserted place and rest a while." Jesus expected His disciples to rest periodically, and He expects us to do the same. This rest renews us and gives us inner peace, enabling us to live our lives at a less hectic pace. When we are at rest, we can better appreciate God and all He does for us. We can focus on the awesome gifts of God's grace—forgiveness and eternal rest. It's very difficult to think about those things while we scurry around physically and mentally. So come aside and rest a while. Or as my grandma would say, "Sit a spell and take a load off your feet."

- *Jeanette Dall*

Lord Jesus, we haven't changed much from the people You and Your disciples watched coming and going. We still spend much of our time scurrying around from one place to another, and even when we are sitting, our minds may be racing with plans and things to do. Help us to come aside and rest a while. Thank You for the perfect rest and peace You give us by Your gift of grace and forgiveness. Amen.

Reflection

Where Are You?

The Lord shall preserve
you from all evil;
He shall preserve your soul.
The Lord shall preserve
your going out and
your coming in
From this time forth,
and even forevermore.

Psalm 121:7–8 (NKJV)

I take care of my two-year-old grandson four days a week. Matthew is at the age when he is starting to assert his independence, but he still wants the security of knowing I'm nearby. Two of Matthew's favorite and oft-repeated phrases illustrate this well. Most of the time Matthew says, "I do it myself!" I hear this when I put him in the car seat, show him how to build a tower of blocks, or anything else Matthew thinks he's capable of doing on his own. I try to be very patient, because I know this is Matthew's way of learning that some things he can do for himself while in other things he still needs help.

"Grammy, where are you?" Matthew calls when he discovers he can't see me. This question is repeated in ever-increasing volume and concern until I answer Matthew or he finds me. Then he smiles and says, "There you are!" Matthew needs to know I'm close by to feel happy, secure, and loved.

Many times we are like two-year-old Matthew. We want to be independent, work out all our problems, and take care of everything ourselves. We may think we don't really need God's help all the time. God is very patient—much more patient than we are—and so He lovingly waits for us to learn about our need for Him. And we do find out that many times we just can't do everything by ourselves, and we end up feeling frustrated and upset. Then we call out for help and say, "God, where are you?"

Our loving and caring God answers, "I'm right here, watching over you and ready to help. Bring all those problems to Me—I'll take care of you." In Psalm 121, the Lord, the Creator, is described as the guardian and protector of His people. God's protection includes every extreme in our lives—light to dark, sun to moon, and everything in between. God never sleeps but watches over His own continuously.

When we remember that God is "preserving our going out and our coming in . . . even forevermore," we can find rest and peace. We can say, "There you are!" with joy and a feeling of security. God's love and ever-present helps warms our innermost souls and hearts with contentment, just as the sun warms the stone of the buildings of Via Casino.

We don't remember how we felt about love and security when we were two years old. But we never outgrow our need for God's untiring watch over our lives—whether we're two or ninety-two.

- *Jeanette Dall*

Caring, loving Father, thank You for being patient with us when we want to assert our independence and "do it ourselves." Thank you for Your untiring watch over our lives and for always being there for us in all circumstances. Help us to joyfully accept the perfect peace You offer us. Amen.

Worried Birds

*Therefore I say to you, do
not worry about your life,
what you will eat or what
you will drink; nor about
your body, what you will
put on. Is not life more than
food and the body more than
clothing? Look at the birds
of the air, for they neither
sow nor reap nor gather into
barns; yet your heavenly
Father feeds them. Are you
not of more value than they?*

Matthew 6:25–26 (NKJV)

As I look at the painting of the Wisteria Arbor, I like to imagine what I would hear if there were a switch to activate the sound. I think I would hear lots of birds singing, chirping, and chatting with their buddies. Some of them might be flitting in and out of the vine, and others would just be enjoying the shade it affords. They would be going about their bird business, not worrying about where the next meal was going to come from.

I've never seen a worried bird—maybe alarmed, bedraggled by rain, or cold from snow—but never worried. In fact, they act as an antidote to worry for me. When I'm fussing and fretting about something, nothing lifts my spirits more quickly than hearing a bird happily singing. The snowiest winter day is made beautiful by the scarlet flash of a cardinal, and winter seems to melt away at the sight of the first robin of the spring.

Birds don't worry, but people do. We worry about things that have happened and things that might happen, big things and little things. We worry about our families, our friends, our neighbors, and the world in general. Some of us are in a constant state of worry, and others of us worry when crises (or imagined crises) occur. There is a difference between worry and genuine concern—worry immobilizes while concern moves us to action.

Because of its ill effects, Jesus tells us not to worry about those needs for which God promises to provide. Worry affects us physically and mentally. It negatively affects the way we treat others and reduces our ability to trust in God. Worry divides, separates, and distracts. One cannot worry and trust God at the same time, because worry destroys the peaceful life God desires for us.

Jesus does not command us not to worry. Rather He reminds us that we are much more valuable than birds. Jesus invites us to rest in the arms of a loving Father. Then we will enjoy that perfect peace and rest that only God can give.

- *Jeanette Dall*

Dearest Jesus, thank You for the lessons that You teach me about simple faith. Help me to learn not to worry but instead to put my trust in You to supply all of my needs. Only You can give me the perfect peace and rest that I desire. In Your good name I pray, Amen.

Index

Notes

1. Dante, Divine Comedy, Paradiso, canto III, l. 85.

2. Saint Francis of Assisi. The Counsels of the Holy Father Saint Francis. Admonition 27.

3. T. S. Eliot, Ash–Wednesday (1930), VI.

    The artwork featured in Perfect Peace and Rest is from Thomas Kinkade's Plein Air collection. Plein air is a French term meaning "open air" and refers to a style of Impressionistic painting created outdoors, giving the artist opportunity to capture the effects light has on a subject at a specific moment in time.